Roger Elliot is one of the best known astrologers in the world today. Through book TV programmes and reputation as an intell future events, with an As a Cancerian he like wife he lives and wo children, dogs and v astrological research a His new book on re available in Granada Paperbacks.

Published by Granada Publishing Limited in 1982

ISBN 0 583 13377 0

A Granada Paperback Original
Copyright © Roger Elliot 1982

Granada Publishing Limited
Frogmore, St Albans, Herts AL2 2NF
and
36 Golden Square, London W1R 4AH
866 United Nations Plaza, New York, NY 10017, USA
117 York Street, Sydney, NSW 2000, Australia
100 Skyway Avenue, Rexdale, Ontario, M9W 3A6, Canada
61 Beach Road, Auckland, New Zealand

Printed and bound in Great Britain by
Cox and Wyman Ltd, Reading
Set in Bembo

Granada ®
Granada Publishing ®

CAPRICORN

★ ★ ★

DECEMBER 22 – JANUARY 20

CONTENTS

MY WORLD OF ASTROLOGY

Once again I welcome you to the beckoning new year – a year, let's hope, that's full of promise and fulfilment for you.

In this book of predictions for 1983 I have tried to pack into one small volume some of the myriad signs and influences that I believe are likely to affect you in the coming year.

As a Capricorn type you respond to life in a cautious but serious-minded way – and won't stand any nonsense! So I must be careful in what I say – otherwise I shall be bombarded with criticism from you!

What does it mean when I say you are a Capricorn person? It means that you were born between December 22 and January 20, a period in the year when the Sun is passing through that patch of the sky known as Capricorn. As a result, you were born with a particular set of characteristics and are liable to pass through life under the influence of these planetary groupings.

Now it stands to reason that not every single Capricornian is identical to his or her fellow Zodiac-members. Even if you were born on the same day of the same year as Fred next door, making you what are known as 'astrological twins', you would still be somewhat different. This is because of family background, inherited qualities, and the different ways in which you and Fred might have been raised. All these factors make some difference.

But it remains demonstrably true that, the closer you are born to Fred, the nearer in temperament you are liable to be. Perhaps you remember a fascinating TV programme a year or two ago in which six astrological twins were gathered together in one studio. These were half a dozen people who had never met before in their lives; they were unrelated, and had nothing in common except their dates of birth.

Well, even to the most hidebound sceptic it would have been obvious that these people, randomly chosen from the population, had a great deal in common. Many looked similar, especially around the eyes; they had the same mannerisms, sometimes the same outlook on life. And what was clear at first sight has subsequently been shown to be true in detailed research: these twins have far more in common than a casually selected sample.

They are *twins of the spirit*, born alike because they were born at the same time – the time when the sky above formed a particular astrological pattern.

This kind of close similarity occurs among people born within hours of each other. But on a broader front it's still possible to gain a good idea of who you are, and where you're going, simply from the heavenly month of your birth – in your case, Capricorn.

Obviously you must use your commonsense when reading my predictions for you. I cannot know all the ins and outs of your daily life – whether you're single or married, in work or on the dole, a youngster or senior citizen.

So you must pick and choose my remarks, deciding for yourself which ones apply to you.

To help you, I've included sections dividing the whole Capricorn family into a number of smaller groupings, according to your age and the particular problem, if any, facing you.

Similarly, in the sign-by-sign analysis of how you harmonize – or conflict – with people from different Zodiac signs, I've included notes on how you get on with parents, children, a boss or a lover from a particular Zodiac sign.

★ ★ ★

Does Astrology Work?

People often ask me how true astrology can be. Does it really indicate the big turning-points in one's life? Can it guide one to make better choices in the future?

Believe me, the answer is 'yes', as I know to my own cost. Let me give you a personal example of what I'm talking about.

A year or so ago, a fire ravaged my beautiful Somerset home. It started, we think, in the loft with a mouse nibbling through an electric cable – and from that tiny animal came a mountain of losses: our house, our furniture and paintings, my books and records and even the computers I use in my astrological research.

Why, asked the TV interviewers, didn't the astrologer predict his own disaster? Well, the truth is that I did – up to a point. There were several indications that month that I would undergo some 'domestic rearrangements'. What's more, I had noticed a particularly dangerous configuration in my young daughter Stephanie's horoscope and had warned her to be careful when crossing roads or swimming – the two activities where I thought she might be at risk. Little did I think that she would escape with her life running at dead of night from her blazing home!

The upshot is clear. I think it unlikely that I – or anyone – can predict *exactly* what will happen in the future. But we can get pretty close.

I, for one, have been taking astrology much more seriously since this fire of ours. The disaster brought home to me, in the most acute way possible, how clearly the pattern of our lives was shown in all my family's horoscopes.

I hope that you will get some help yourself from this little Capricorn book, which I offer you in all sincerity as a possible guide to your future. If you want to know more about your life, I suggest that you obtain your individual Birthday Horoscope mentioned on p. 64.

In the meantime, I wish you good luck and happy landings in your journey through 1983!

ROGER ELLIOT

YOUR YEAR AHEAD

This seems quite a public-spirited year for you. You may be in the public eye, if only in a small way, or helping to run a charity, voluntary service or social club. This is particularly emphasised early in the year; February is full of activities, and so is May. In between, your home life becomes prominent, with something to celebrate in March and a worry on behalf of a relative over Easter. Your own marriage (existing or intended) comes into sharp relief in June. If you were planning to wed, all goes well; if already married, you could find that there's a make-or-break phase this midsummer. If looking for someone new, the hoped-for romance will develop through the long, hot summer, when there are signs that you'll be much more free and open than usual. There are special links with Aquarians and Scorpians, incidentally. August could be financially lucky, especially if you're a gambling beginner. September is more sombre, with the possibility of bad news within the family circle. Alternatively if you are hoping to move house, there may be a disappointment, though a move will eventually take place. October is full of money worries, with people asking you for cash and perhaps a failure to gain promotion or a pay rise. But November seems jollier; you may have a new part-time job that is more of a hobby. December brings old friends back into your life, and it's a great month for a holiday away from home.

★ ★ ★
Your Strengths in 1983 . . .

Your main strength in the coming year seems to be your public-spiritedness, at least in the first half of 1983.

You're aware that you have a role to play in the community, and with your usual Capricorn efficiency you will set about playing that role in a strong and capable manner.

Obviously you get a personal kick out of this; but there's also a sense of service and charity which is most gratifying to see.

Another strength, I believe, comes in mid-year, when you drop your slightly haughty Capricorn outlook on life and relax a great deal. This is most likely going to be linked, for many Capricorn folk, with an exciting love affair; but even if it isn't, you'll still be a pleasure-loving, hedonistic sort of person for a few months. It will do you so much good.

★ ★ ★
. . . and Weaknesses

One weakness, I suppose, is your slyness which may be apparent later in the year. At the time, I think you'll see this as a strength, however. But whatever excuse you make, in the end it will be a kind of hypocrisy – telling white lies, saying one thing and meaning another, keeping a secret from some-one who ought to know.

Another weakness is a tendency, always at the back of the Capricorn mind, towards depression when things get a bit grim. This is particularly apparent in the autumn months when there may be one or two strokes of bad luck.

Finally, I might mention your weakness for sticking a bit too rigidly to the rules at times. You won't in the summer, but at the beginning and end of the year you'll be obeying the letter but not the spirit of the law.

★ ★ ★
What Makes 1983 Different?

The unique quality about 1983, which distinguishes it quite clearly from any year in your life up till now, is the entry of Pluto, late in 1983, into your Eleventh Solar House.

This won't affect you all year, but the pattern of your life is building up towards it. It suggests that there could be a big make-or-break phase in one particular friendship (not neces-sarily romance) and that you might soon (in the next year or two) be 'converted' to a new belief or political point of view.

THE SEVEN AGES
OF CAPRICORN

Although you were born under the sign of Capricorn and remain a Capricornian all your life, you react to its influence in different ways – according to your age. Here is your special guide to 1983 based on the age-group you belong to.

★ ★ ★
New-Born Babies

This includes babies due to be born in the course of 1983, plus those who have arrived in the last year or two.

Capricorn children are often slow developers. It takes time for their true personalities to emerge. They are happier in their middle years than in their youth, but their upbringing can have a crucial effect on their adult years.

As infants, Capricornians are rather shy and reserved. If they are slow at walking and talking, don't worry – they like to progress at their own steady pace.

All their lives they will be loners, to some extent, but that doesn't mean that they don't need a lot of sensible encouragement. They often take after their fathers rather than their mothers, and certainly the paternal influence is often more powerful. They need a figure of authority to whom they can respond.

As infants they may sleep a lot, but they also go through anxious periods when they fret, for little or no reason. They like the company of other babies, but are as easy mixers as they could be.

★ ★ ★
Children

This includes children from the age of three to twelve.

They enjoy being trusted, being given practical jobs around the house, and above all earning privileges through good behaviour.

From quite an early age, they should be allowed to choose how they spend their own pocket-money; and under the right guidance they will soon develop a sound financial common-sense.

This year they are particularly shrewd and sensible.

★★★
Teenagers

Capricorn teenagers grow up fast in one way; they almost seem middle-aged before they're even grown up! But in another way they awaken relatively slowly to the world around them.

They are capable of achieving a fine academic record, especially in science, mathematics and history. In the coming year they are likely to fall in love – perhaps for the first time – through the summer of '83. But they retain enough wisdom to continue their schooling through to college.

★★★
Young Adults

This includes all young Capricorn men and women in their twenties and early thirties.

This looks a fulfilling year for most of them. They may not enjoy the promotion at work that they think they deserve, but they make steady progress in other areas.

If they are still unmarried, this could easily be the year when they fall in love and wed. If they married too young, however, 1983 could mark the start of infidelity.

They will enjoy family life, and get on well with their parents and in-laws.

★★★
Prime of Life

Broadly speaking, this group includes all Capricornians in their late thirties and forties.

Capricorn people in this age-group are beginning to feel

truly at home in the world. They should have achieved quite a bit already; but the best is yet to come.

1983 suits them tolerably well. They will enjoy the political and charitable work that comes their way. Their jobs, too, should be fairly interesting, though they run the danger of getting in a rut when they should be moving forward.

★ ★ ★
Middle Age

This applies to all Capricornians in their fifties and early sixties.

This is a good year for them to be breaking fresh ground, having become rather stick-in-the-mud in the last few years. For many of them, a romance will flourish. There will be money problems, especially if their partner's finances are worse than they thought.

Divorcees of either sex stand a good chance of remarrying this year. Make the most of it, because Capricorn people remarry least of all the Zodiac signs.

★ ★ ★
Senior Citizens

Finally I come to Capricorn people over the age of sixty-five.

Their health will stand up pretty well during 1983. They will want to tackle something artistic or creative, even if they've never tried their hand at anything like that before.

They could be sleeping badly in mid-year. They will be distressed at the behaviour of some young people. They will be more emotional than usual, and may start telling some home truths for the first time ever!

IS THIS YOUR PROBLEM?

You may be facing a specially difficult problem at the moment – one that worries you a great deal and seems to be the biggest obstacle to happiness in your life.

If so, here are a few words of comfort and advice that may help you through this troublesome dilemma.

★ ★ ★
Looking for Love

Many Capricorn folk, although they have many admirable qualities, sometimes have difficulties in relating easily to other people.

Partly it's a question of shyness and reserve. You find it hard to make trivial relationships; you are always looking for a long-term, meaningful partnership.

The chances are that 1983 will furnish you with an exciting and passionate love affair, though I cannot promise that it will last forever.

However you will respond to the break-up, if it comes, remains to be seen; but at least you should find some affection this year.

★ ★ ★
Running Your Own Business

You are a capable administrator, with a lot of drive and determination. You can make hard decisions, but you are less good at co-operating with others or creating a warm and happy work-force under you.

The particular difficulties in 1983 will be:

(1) A fear that you will be let down by government policy and decisions. Although world trade is improving, your government may not be as positive as you'd wish.

(2) Production difficulties, especially if you are introducing a new range. You may be too fussy over packaging, and possibly you'll price yourself out the market.

★★★
Ill-Health

1983 should be a better year for health than you've enjoyed for quite a long time.

Obviously if you have a chronic illness I cannot promise that it will disappear overnight. Equally a physical or mental disability will remain with you; but I feel you'll be able to cope better, and enjoy life more, despite the difficulties facing you.

The likelihood of any new serious illness developing is certainly less in 1983 than previously.

★★★
I'm a Failure!

It's perilously easy for the Capricorn person to feel himself a failure. You are a born pessimist, and like looking on the gloomy side!

Actually you are capable of being a realist rather than pessimist. You have high standards, and when you don't reach them you feel worse than most people would.

My best advice is to relax and enjoy yourself more. This is certainly the pattern shown to be developing through the summer months of 1983, when a more pleasure-loving approach to life will be evident. You won't care so much about being a success.

★★★
In the Wrong Job

If you are deeply unhappy in your present job, there are two moments in 1983 when a change may be attempted: around springtime and again in October or November.

There is no guarantee that you'll be successful in the sense of finding the perfect employment. You have a good aptitude for administration of all kinds. You have a special feeling for the past, so any job that involves history, antiques, restoration or maintaining traditions is okay for you.

You are also good at teaching, law and order, the armed services and heavy engineering.

★ ★ ★

Problems in Marriage

You are a long-term creature in the sense that you want a marriage to last forever.

This makes it very hard for you to forgive a partner who wants a divorce. you fight against the notion, even though the logical side of your nature might agree that it's the best solution.

There are no obvious signs of a break-up this year. If anything, I think you could have a lively and unconventional liaison with someone younger and more trivially-minded than yourself, but that in the end you'll remain married.

Obviously there will be exceptions, but that's the overall tendency for married Capricornians in 1983.

MIXING WITH OTHERS

One of the most valuable uses of astrology lies in the field of personal relationships. By knowing the characteristics of your Sun-sign Capricorn you get a good idea of your own personality; and by knowing about other Zodiac signs as well you can grasp how well – or badly! – you harmonize with other folk.

Zodiac signs can be grouped in a variety of ways. There are the Elements (the familiar Earth, Air, Fire and Water) and the Modes. You can see at a glance which Element and Mode you – and your friends – belong to.

ELEMENTS	MODES		
	CARDINAL	FIXED	MUTABLE
FIRE	Aries	Leo	Sagittarius
EARTH	Capricorn	Taurus	Virgo
AIR	Libra	Aquarius	Gemini
WATER	Cancer	Scorpio	Pisces

FIRE signs need excitement and glamour out of life. They wake up other people, sometimes burn them up. They have great enthusiasm.

EARTH signs are down-to-earth folk. They enjoy being practical and dependable. They need to be constructive, but can be sluggish companions.

AIR signs are breezy, sociable people. They enjoy most

company, but need plenty of variety in life. They love exchanging ideas and gossip.

WATER signs are tender, sympathetic creatures. They can flow into other people's hearts and minds, but are often on the defensive, too.

CARDINAL signs like to accomplish things in life. Give them a problem and they want to solve it. They like a relationship to progress.

FIXED signs like to maintain an existing situation. They can prove marvellously faithful . . . and terribly obstinate! Not very adaptable.

MUTABLE signs like to keep their options open. They prefer variety to monotony, and are not very dependable! But they can wriggle out of problems.

Fire and Air signs are meant to get along particularly well, for they feed off each other's ideas and enthusiasm. Similarly Earth and Water people have much in common, for they can fertilize each other in a growing relationship.

Other combinations present difficulties. Take Fire and Water; it can be a sizzling relationship at first, but Water can also dampen Fire's ardour. Or Earth and Air: together they can produce a dustbowl, a whirlwind of arid sand. Air and Water, meanwhile, resemble the bubbles of a fizzy drink: intoxicating to start with, but tending to go their own separate ways.

None of this means that some combinations are unsuitable for each other and should never associate together. On the contrary, most marriages are formed between people who are different from each other. One partner supplies the personal qualities that the other lacks. Gradually, through trial and error, they become a true couple – a mixture of their Zodiac signs made through compromise, tolerance and love. There's often a mixture of Modes, too, so that a Cardinal husband is active in the outside world while a Fixed wife busies herself keeping the home and family in good order. Marriage is like cookery: any kind of ingredients can make a wonderful dish.

In the next few pages, you can see how you will fare in 1983.

★ ★ ★
Aries (March 21 to April 20) **and You**

Aries and Capricorn aren't meant to go together; but in real life you can make a formidable team, especially as a husband-and-wife team in business together.

You both have a realistic outlook. At worst, Capricorn can be too earthy and stolid for lively Aries – while Aries can seem far too impulsive to cautious Capricorn.

In 1983 there are no special links drawing you closer or pushing you apart.

With an ARIES PARENT you can swing him or her round to your point of view: especially to do with an out-of-the-way topic.

If you have an ARIES CHILD things should be proceeding happily enough: no real change, in fact, since 1982. I feel you can enjoy each other's company better, now he's older.

If your ARIES BOSS goes through an indecisive mood, you can provide the strength of character to see him through.

Finally, with an ARIES LOVER remember that the relationship grows month by month, year by year. Don't be in a hurry.

★ ★ ★
Taurus (April 21 to May 21) **and You**

This is an admirable, strong, solid combination. You may not like each other straight away, but once the link is formed it cannot be easily broken.

Other people may find you a tough, hard-headed couple. In 1983 this business acumen will be paramount. It's an ideal time to be starting a new venture together, or battling through a period of worry. In a new romance, too, there may be some initial problems before you can get properly together.

A TAUREAN PARENT can provide you with material comforts and emotional assurance. But you have ambitions beyond them.

A TAUREAN CHILD has a no-nonsense kind of relationship with you in 1983. You will work and play happily together.

With a TAUREAN BOSS the same applies. It's a pleasant kind of liaison, without demands or fuss.

A TAUREAN LOVER will be amorous and sexy, but can be a bit mean where money is concerned.

★ ★ ★
Gemini (May 22 to June 21) **and You**

Gemini and Capricorn are meant to be poles apart – and yet in a funny way you are nicely complementary to each other. So there are dangers in the relationship . . . but opportunities too.

If you think of your relationship as a sail-boat, Gemini is the sail and Capricorn the anchor. Although very different, each needs the other.

The outlook for 1983 is broadly good. Gemini must not allow Capricorn to be too stick-in-the-mud.

If you have a GEMINI PARENT there may be minor flashes of temper; but on the whole it's a good year together.

With a GEMINI CHILD there's a restlessness and lack of application that worries you.

If you have a GEMINI BOSS you'll see the same sort of thing. You are the one who has to do all the routine tasks.

Your GEMINI LOVER enjoys your company, but may not get on well with your family.

★ ★ ★
Cancer (June 22 to July 22) **and You**

Cancer and Capricorn are at opposite ends of the Zodiac, but this doesn't mean that you are totally poles apart. On the contrary, you suit each other. In combination you form a somewhat careful, conservative couple who will become increasingly set in your ways as you get older.

Indeed, the older you are the happier you'll be. Brand-new romances between these signs take time to get off the ground, and this is particularly true in 1983.

With a CANCER PARENT you place a lot of reliance on his or her advice and comfort, especially a Cancer father.

Towards a CANCER CHILD you have deep ties, but these are not always comfortable.

If you have a CANCER BOSS you make a good team at work, but he may be a little in awe of you.

A CANCER LOVER is fearful of sacrificing some of his or her independence. Don't be too possessive and restrictive.

★ ★ ★
Leo (July 23 to August 23) **and You**

Here are two power-seeking Zodiac signs, and it's easy for a Leo-Capricorn marriage to turn into a battle for dominance. But you use different weapons. The Capricorn person can be a profoundly cynical, worldly-wise type, whereas Leo always retains some measure of innocence.

The differences are not so pronounced in 1983, and together you can achieve a good deal. You will be admired by others, and may even receive some kind of honour or recognition.

If you have a LEO PARENT you will be urged to enjoy yourself more. But you are working steadily towards a goal.

With a LEO CHILD you can do well as a team. Perhaps you will win a joint prize.

A LEO BOSS is intelligent and shrewd, but you don't think he really brings out the best in you.

Finally, a LEO LOVER wants to take charge of the relationship from the word go. Quite a battle for dominance!

★ ★ ★
Virgo (August 24 to September 22) **and You**

Two Earth signs like Capricorn and Virgo should have little difficulty in establishing a loving rapport. But in a way it's more a business partnership than an affectionate one.

It improves with age. Together you can form a stable, long-lasting union, but because both of you like work, you like to see your marriage as a partnership for doing things together.

In 1983 there will be opportunities to make money together.

If you have a VIRGO PARENT there's a danger that he or she will try to baby you too much. The relationship should now be on an equal footing.

With a VIRGO CHILD there's respect and quiet progress.

A VIRGO BOSS is a bit fearful of change. But there's one improvement you are keen to put into effect.

A VIRGO LOVER is a friend as much as a bed-partner. Cultivate this friendship, and you'll stay together a long time.

★ ★ ★

Libra (September 23 to October 23) and You

On the face of it there's a large difference in temperament here. The Capricorn partner will be much more dogmatic, ambitious and hard-working than the Libran type, while Libra in turn seems superficially more loving and affectionate.

But there are subtle, underlying links between these Zodiac signs suggesting that you can achieve a fine rapport together.

In 1983 you will get on better than usual. Respect is vital, so try not to treat Libra as a machine instead of a human being!

With a LIBRA PARENT you may be criticised for working too hard and not having enough fun.

If you have a LIBRA CHILD you may be too disciplined. It's important that you show your love openly. Be more demonstrative.

With a LIBRA BOSS you will get angry if not enough work gets done.

If you have a LIBRA LOVER the relationship will flower in a slow, gentle but harmonious way.

★ ★ ★

Scorpio (October 24 to November 22) and You

This is a relationship with every intention of lasting until death do you part! But it's one that may not flourish too easily in the early stages. You can grow together better than almost any other Zodiac combination, and it can remain a power struggle.

Business will go well under your joint aegis, but emotional problems could abound in 1983, with Scorpio edgy and Capricorn too smug and self-satisfied.

The coming year is not an easy time for either of you.

With a SCORPIO PARENT there are certain items in your private life that you simply don't want to discuss.

The same applies to a SCORPIO CHILD, only this time it's the child who will be secretive.

A SCORPIO BOSS has a clear idea how he wants things done. Woe betide you if you disagree – as I think you will in 1983.

A SCORPIO LOVER may admire you from afar – and fail to let you know how he or she really feels about you.

★ ★ ★
Sagittarius (November 23 to December 21) and You

Here there's a fundamental difference of temperament. Capricorn people tend to hang on through thick and thin, while Sagittarius is a lot more versatile . . . and inconsistent!

Capricorn likes to know exactly where he stands. Sagittarius enjoys the spice of surprise and adventure.

The differences are strongly marked in 1983. If Capricorn can't keep up with Sagittarius's pace, they will get further and further apart.

With a SAGITTARIUS PARENT you can get a great deal of fun. He or she can lift you from your occasional depressions.

With a SAGITTARIUS CHILD there is a great temptation for you to quieten him down. Give the boy (or girl) a bit of freedom.

A SAGITTARIUS BOSS is a tremendous inspiration this year, though nine out of ten ideas are wrong-headed – one is brilliant!

Finally, with a SAGITTARIUS LOVER you may not be the only one in his or her life. This will make you jealous and insecure.

★ ★ ★
Capricorn (December 22 to January 20) and You

The Capricorn tendency is to put up a defensive outer personality. At worst, you can both be defensive towards each other and never really get inside each other's shell to form a true rapport.

But once formed, this link is very hard to break – it survives crises, disasters and the ravages of age!

The outlook in 1983 is fairly promising. You will enjoy each other's company, and find success together.

This is specially true with a CAPRICORN PARENT. It could be the start of a new lease of life for both of you.

A CAPRICORN CHILD will do specially well in one particular area of life, filling you with pride.

A CAPRICORN BOSS, meanwhile, may be under threat from higher management. If so, you may not stay with him.

Remember that with a CAPRICORN LOVER you understand each other only too well. A bit of variety would do you good.

★ ★ ★

Aquarius (January 21 to February 18) **and You**

You are basically similar creatures, but whereas the Aquarian is outward, experimental and idealistic, the Capricorn person is more introspective, practical and realistic.

Given goodwill you can understand each other's motives. But there's strong rivalry as well.

This year, however, you are being driven by somewhat different impulses. Capricorn is in a quiet, steady mood, while Aquarius is much more lively and go-getting.

In 1983 an AQUARIUS PARENT will get impatient with you. It may be that this won't be your most favourite relative this year!

With an AQUARIUS CHILD there is harmony in small doses. If you spend too much time together, the relationship will get stale.

If you have an AQUARIUS BOSS there may be talk of moving elsewhere – but in the end I guess you'll stay together.

An AQUARIUS LOVER wants more out of life than mere romance. Get involved in his or her interests if you want to stay together.

★ ★ ★

Pisces (February 19 to March 20) **and You**

There's a gulf of difference between your two temperaments. But you can develop a great fondness for each other.

Capricorn will always tend to be the leader, but actually can learn much from the tender Piscean soul.

At worst there's an air of melancholy between you, as though each one is disappointed in the other but too kindly to do anything drastic about it! But with a bit of luck, this depressing attitude won't be so apparent in 1983.

This is true of a PISCES PARENT who may be a bit neurotic about life in general. You aren't much good at cheering people up.

A PISCES CHILD needs fresh outlets. Try and encourage him or her to venture into new pastures in social life.

From a PISCES BOSS you receive delays, procrastination and a lot of sympathy when things go badly with you.

With a PISCES LOVER you could have a wonderful few months together – but you find it tempting to bully this sweetheart.

MONTH-BY-MONTH PLANNING GUIDE

JANUARY
Your Monthly Guide

You·start the year in a surprisingly public-spirited manner. This may be in politics, trades union affairs or local organisation devoted to charity and good works.

You aren't in an arrogant mood, but you are certainly ambitious. You'll want to make a big effort this year, as though you've made some determined New Year resolutions which you're keen to keep.

Don't expect everyone to agree with you, though. If you develop an individual plan of action, you'll have a job explaining it to others – and convincing them that it's the right course to pursue, especially if money is involved.

So January looks eager, energetic but a bit solitary.

WORK. At work the mood is a bit sombre. There could be an industrial dispute hovering – either in your own workplace or somewhere else. Either way, it will affect your own employment, with the danger of some Capricorns getting laid off for a while and others, perhaps in management or their own company, desperately trying to make ends meet.

If you work in the retail trade, the January sales will be worse than ever! If you're employed in one of the professions – the law especially – there could be a surprise skeleton in a cupboard about to rattle its bones in public.

HOME. Home life is fairly amiable, though there will be some disagreements within the family circle. One matter being discussed could be the future career of a youngster. You will have fairly clearcut ideas, based on your own experience or the traditions of your side of the family. Your marriage partner, not to mention the young person concerned, will have very different ideas, though they can't express them as well as yourself.

If yours is a musical household, there could be some pleasant evenings making music together. This is specially true if a new instrument – say an electronic organ – formed someone's Christmas present recently.

HEALTH. Your health should be pretty stable, you'll be glad to hear. Capricorn people are often prone to chills and colds, but I've a hunch you'll get through this winter with few, if any, days in bed.

If you have a chronic illness, it should be giving relatively little pain at the moment. If it's a disease that comes and goes, such as multiple sclerosis, you should start 1983 with your strength and mobility on the increase.

MONEY. For some Capricorn folk there will be a heavy drain on your resources in early 1983.

You may be giving some money to a worthy cause – either as cash or as services rendered. If you have anything to do with an amateur show, performance or exhibition, you'll be out of pocket buying materials.

There will also be extra expense to do with a motor car, van or bicycle. Something major will have to be replaced, at considerable cost.

If you want a gamble, there are several promising dates. On the whole you do better following carefully selected favourites than promising outsiders.

LEISURE. A lot of leisure time could be taken up with some public work. You may possibly be speaking in public – or acting, singing, etc. if you're a performer.

There will also be a lot of fun entertaining children, especially if the weather is unusual. A visit to a newly redesigned museum will be very instructive.

One dinner date that you've been looking forward to will have to be cancelled. A weekend away will go ahead okay, but in rather different circumstances than planned.

LOVE. It's a caring, sharing start to your romantic year. With your regular partner you'll share some happy moments

26

together. With a brand-new love affair there'll be a lot of tenderness and sympathy – more, in fact, than sexuality, so that the physical side of the relationship may be slow to get off the ground.

The middle of January is a bit of a doldrums, as far as love is concerned. Your mind will be on other matters, and you won't be able to work up as much desire as you should.

Nice links with Taureans and Librans at the moment.

KEY DATES THIS MONTH

Saturday 1st: You need to say goodbye to the past. Excellent day for making a tentative proposal, to see how it goes.

Monday 3rd: Take care of your health by all means, but don't fuss unduly. Back at work you'll find a surprise awaiting you.

Wednesday 5th: You will enjoy a meal out, and may make some new acquaintances.

Friday 7th: A youngster will be hopeful, and needs your encouragement. Lucky numbers: 5, 14.

Saturday 8th: It may be slow going today. Machinery may go wrong, making you late for an appointment or special event. The evening looks quiet.

Sunday 9th: It will be a lazy morning, but you must move fast in the afternoon.

Thursday 13th: Next-door neighbours will be friendly, and will lend a hand if you're in a squeeze.

Friday 14th: A friend wants you to take part in a special event later this month. It may involve making a fool of yourself.

Sunday 16th: You are in a responsible frame of mind. You'll want to stop a young person from taking the wrong road.

Wednesday 19th: You seem more cheerful than usual. Perhaps you'll be lucky with money. Lucky numbers: 7, 20.

Saturday 22nd: Use your charm if you think it will work! But you're stronger on commonsense!

Tuesday 25th: Take your time before reaching a decision. Someone is hurrying you to make a snap choice.

Thursday 27th: There's less to do than you expect. Someone could be trying to interfere with your private life.

Saturday 29th: A lovely weekend. You should be in a happy mood, with the pleasure of meeting someone again whom you knew some time ago.

FEBRUARY
Your Monthly Guide

Your own life is pretty normal, but all sorts of excitement could be happening in the lives of people around you.

Obviously you'll want to give sympathy and understanding, especially if one of the persons involved is part of the close family circle. But this won't, in itself, be enough. I think you'll have to give some practical help, even in matters that you know little about.

In one area of life – work or a hobby, perhaps – a special effort now will achieve a kind of breakthrough. You may have to tackle a familiar problem in a brand-new way, which is unusual for you, a normally cautious and careful individual. But the results will make the risk well worth taking.

WORK. No big developments. Indeed, one of your complaints may be that a hoped-for promotion will not materialise – for a while, at least. A project at work may be delayed or cancelled for lack of funds.

You may have to accept some temporary extra responsibility, due to illness or a training course for others or simply a cutting-down of staff levels. This is obviously a chance to impress your boss with your efficiency, but you'll see it as a bit of a liberty.

You'll find that a skill learnt quite a while ago will come in handy again.

HOME. Your home life remains pretty settled. There should be some encouraging news about a youngster at school or training college. It may involve extra money from you, to help pay for more tuition or a longer stay at college.

It's a wise time to be planning changes in the garden, even if it's too cold in Britain to be putting them into effect straight away. You will probably want to compartmentalize the garden in some way, which could include putting in hedges, a pergola, a screen or similar device.

You may also want to help an elderly relative with an aspect of life he or she can no longer deal with adequately. This could involve a weekend's work helping to get things straight.

HEALTH. Mid-month could be a slightly difficult time for you. A swollen throat and larynx is one possibility, especially if you speak a lot in the course of your job. If you suffer from bronchitis anyway, this could crop up during February.

Even so, I think you'll get through the winter in pretty good shape. If you live in a warmer climate than Britain's, there is a danger of a tropical virus laying you low for a while.

There could be some trouble with teeth. If you haven't seen your dentist for a while, book an appointment. You may well have inflamed gums that will benefit from a course of treatment from a dental hygienist.

MONEY. You are still having to pay out to keep other people happy: one family dependant, in particular.

If you were hoping to afford a big new item of expenditure in the home – such as a new bathroom or kitchen – I fear this purchase will have to be put off until April.

If you like playing the Stock Market, there could be some shares in a company that has recently been diversifying a great deal that will yield a quick profit.

As a gambler, you will do best with second favourites early in February. Later in the month there could be a moment of luck on the pools – but I'm not promising you first dividend on the Treble Chance!

LEISURE. You could be getting ready for springtime activities when the weather gets warmer. If you own a caravan, now's the time to give it a thorough overhaul and perhaps interior redecoration.

If you own greyhounds, whippets or racing pigeons, there could be a danger from allowing your animals to mix with others. It's only temporary, but it could be an infection.

Social life is relatively quiet this month. People can't afford to entertain much. You owe a number of people invitations back, and you could have a fairly modest evening entertaining at home.

LOVE. A very quiet month in romance. You aren't very dynamic in your approach. Whatever love-making takes place will be relatively fond, relatively relaxing, and relatively pleasant!

Wednesday 2nd: Nice surprise around the corner. If away from home, there could be a meeting that makes you realize it's a small world.

Friday 4th: Something will get lost, causing anxiety over the weekend. Too much drink will do you no good at all!

Sunday 6th: A phone call will bring happiness. A late night seems indicated – or perhaps you can't sleep.

Wednesday 9th: There could be a disappointment to do with home. A friend will cheer you up, and there could be a surprise in the evening.

Sunday 13th: Plenty of vigorous exercise is what you need. But you would prefer to avoid someone, who may phone or pay a visit.

Wednesday 16th: Quite a lucky day. Lucky colour will be red.

Friday 18th: You worry about a child who may be acting in a slightly abnormal way.

Saturday 19th: A nice moment of sentimentality will make your day. You are full of love and affection.

Monday 21st: You must cope with an unexpected surprise. Don't get too optimistic; things are more likely to go wrong than right.

Wednesday 23rd: Fine day for romance, with a touch of nostalgia thrown in. There could be contact with showbusiness at some stage this week.

Friday 25th: Don't take 'no' from anyone – because it isn't the right answer. Keep badgering away, and you'll start to hear what you want.

Saturday 26th: What should be signed, sealed and delivered will start to seem doubtful. This will be particularly worrying if you're trying to buy or sell property.

Monday 28th: You have got used to one state of affairs. Now the pattern is getting upset.

★ ★ ★

MARCH
Your Monthly Guide

There could be something special to celebrate this month. It could be a family anniversary that brings different branches of the family closer together.

Or, at work, it could be the promotion or better job that you've been hoping for. Obviously this could apply to yourself or your spouse.

Alternatively, within your social life there could be some special event which calls for celebration. If you've been active in public affairs for some years, you could receive a local honour or recognition.

It seems as though this celebration won't have a great deal to do with the general run of your daily life.

WORK. If you do get a new job, or a better chance to flourish in the one you've got, you'll be full of drive and enthusiasm. This is specially true, of course, if you've been out of work for some time. You'll see this opportunity as the chance to make good, after a stale and unprofitable period of laziness.

Two other points to watch for:

(1) Working conditions may not be so easy. There could be building repairs taking place that make your office or factory-floor a dusty and uncomfortable place for a while.

(2) There could be the glimmerings of an office romance, whatever your age! I suggest that this brief flurry of desire will not lead anywhere significant. Forget it!

HOME. There's a big emphasis on your family life. Perhaps there's a special wedding anniversary to celebrate, or the success of a relative in a particular field of study, sport or career.

I think there will be quite a large get-together, either at your place or else at someone else's home some distance away.

If you are considering an extension or loft conversion soon, think again. The expense will be considerable, and there are several practical problems to which there's no easy solution.

There could be a breakage, tear or accident in the home that will make some old, out-of-date furnishings need to be replaced. Hurrah!

HEALTH. A pretty good month. If you get the chance to have a medical check-up, either on the firm or through an insurance company or whatever, seize the opportunity. Nothing serious will be found, and it will set everyone's mind at rest. This is particularly important if you've been betraying slight but potentially alarming symptoms recently – say to do with the heart.

MONEY. You won't spend a great deal this month, partly because you'll be able to persuade your marriage partner not to spend!

You may even be able to save a little extra, or there could be a small windfall sum coming your way.

This could be a backdated pay settlement, for instance, a tax rebate or even an inheritance. This year's Budget will also contain some good news for you.

Capricorn gamblers should enjoy a little luck in a totally unskilled pastime such as roulette or bingo.

LEISURE. A friendly month when you'll be mixing with others a lot more than you've managed to date.

If you belong to a local club, you'll have some good evenings there. If it's a sports club of any kind, you'll have a special victory to celebrate.

Friends will visit from another part of the country, and you'll promise to pay a return visit later in the year.

Educational matters will go with a swing. If you're attending any evening classes, they will be specially fascinating at this time. Some Capricorn people will be starting to take an interesting correspondence course around now.

LOVE. Quite a pleasant month. There's one thing you must watch, though. As a Capricorn type you can be rather bossy at times, and this may not make you the perfect companion!

The start of March is a busy time, and you may not have much time or energy for romance. But by the second half of the month you'll have more time to relax, and the chance of getting away together for a few days shouldn't be missed.

Within a happy relationship there will be some little quarrels, but they won't amount to much.

KEY DATES THIS MONTH

Tuesday 1st: You get a lucky break, making contact with the right people. But you could also be feeling ill.

Thursday 3rd: Companions are more cheerful than you. Don't spend all day on chores that get you nowhere.

Saturday 5th: A bit of luck will come your way. Follow your own hunches, never mind what others say.

Monday 7th: Trouble at work. It could be an industrial dispute. You may hear the result of a test.

Thursday 10th: A visit to another home will open your eyes in surprise. Make sure you don't leave your belongings in the wrong place – or shopping left on the counter!

Saturday 12th: Not a nice weekend. There could be a problem to which there's no obvious solution. Your love life could get in a muddle, too.

Tuesday 15th: Today will be more fun than you expect. You could be on tenterhooks waiting to hear something.

Thursday 17th: You could discover an artful little dodge – a way of taking a short cut, perhaps.

Saturday 19th: A friend will dither, so you'll be kept waiting. If you're in business, it could be a busy weekend fixing up a deal.

Monday 21st: More business on your mind. A visit to the bank manager may be necessary.

Tuesday 22nd: Quite lucky, provided you don't expect to win each race on the card! Lucky numbers: 2 and 10.

Friday 25th: Don't let a moaner get you down. If you play sport, this could be a marvellous weekend.

Saturday 26th: Someone may misunderstand your motives – but never mind, you end up the winner.

Sunday 27th: The children will be much on your mind. There could be a row brewing – over nothing really!

★★★
APRIL
Your Monthly Guide

You will feel under pressure this month. Partly it's the circumstances around you, but mainly it's your own mood.

You are more short-tempered than usual, quicker to take offence when none was intended. And you're inclined to over-react, jumping to the wrong conclusions too hastily.

In other words, you want to be left alone to get on with your own life, without being hurried or pushed around by others. The wise thing, from their point of view, will be to leave you alone.

Partly your edgy mood could be caused by uncertainty about someone else's feelings for you.

WORK. You seem unable to leave your work behind you, when you go home at night. It may be a question of working overtime, or finding that your work-schedule interferes with your family life.

If you run your own business, or have a position of responsibility, you could have insomnia worrying about the future.

This is a good time for Capricorn people to take a second part-time evening job – one that you can do at home or in the immediate neighbourhood.

At all events, there's an atmosphere of work at home, which could be encouraged by children preparing for the summer exams.

HOME. You get some fun entertaining at home this month, but it must be done on your terms, not other people's. You will worry about the appearance of the place, especially if you've changed home recently, but won't find it easy to establish the right, easy charm.

An elderly relative will be in your thoughts at Easter. This could mark the end of a difficult phase of life for this person. Things will be better from now on.

Redecorating tasks go well, and working together with a neighbour will make you better friends. But if anyone starts taking liberties with you, you'll get very knotted-up and solitary.

HEALTH. You're moving from a sociable to a quieter and perhaps more vulnerable phase of life.

Your energy in the past few months has kept you pretty fit and wide-awake. Now, with greater sensitivity and less outward activity, you may become prone to more imbalance within your body.

Capricorn people are often taken by surprise when they fall ill. You put up a big unconscious barrier against illness. When the barrier breaks, you're amazed how quickly a virus can overtake you.

MONEY. Your financial affairs could get into a muddle almost overnight and you may have to do what someone else says in order to get them right.

It's possible that this muddle could be caused by a theft – not necessarily of money or valuables as such, but perhaps of papers, bills, cheque-books or credit cards. So do be careful – as you could waste a lot of time for a moment of forgetfulness, especially in the midst of a busy, efficient day.

A child's pocket-money, or young person's allowance, is also a matter for serious consideration. It may be a good idea to raise the sum quite a bit, but ensure that the child concerned gives a proper account of how the money is spent, especially if a clothes allowance is involved.

LEISURE. You may be spending several evenings or weekends going over to see a relative about whom you're concerned.

I've indicated that basically this is a quiet month for you. You're not wildly unfriendly, unless someone puts the needle in, but you'd prefer to be left alone to enjoy your leisure hours in your own way.

LOVE. You could start to feel that all is not entirely well with the relationship you're 'enjoying' at the moment.

You are being hyper-critical, remember, of yourself as well as your partner. And possibly a degree of fantasy is involved; the grass always seems greener on the other side of the valley, as the saying goes.

Well, you may be pining for someone who slipped out of your grasp some time ago.

KEY DATES THIS MONTH

Friday 1st: An edgy day when people behave in an unpredictable manner. You're so busy with little things that something important could be forgotten.
Sunday 3rd: A muddled day. You have a lazy morning, followed by a bustle in the afternoon.

Monday 4th: Queues will annoy you today. If out and about, you stay cheerful, even if the family is whining!

Thursday 7th: Take trouble over the start of anything new. Get details right. Don't be slapdash – as if a Capricorn would!

Saturday 9th: A jollier weekend than you've enjoyed for some time. You are lucky at the end of the afternoon. The evening deserves a touch of glamour.

Tuesday 12th: In business you'll be sold a pup, if you're not canny. You worry about someone close to you – but you can't control his or her life, so don't bother to try.

Thursday 14th: The warmer weather will cheer you up. There could be nice news about a holiday this summer.

Saturday 16th: Romance beckons. You feel very romantic, but you must make an effort yourself if you want to give happiness.

Monday 18th: Events at the weekend will still be much on your mind. Your guess is as good as anyone's – but an expert opinion still has a lot going for it!

Wednesday 20th: There could be medical news to hear. A slip on the stairs could send things flying!

Thursday 21st: Introduce humour into a heavy atmosphere. You can control an important meeting through your quiet force of character.

Tuesday 26th: Money matters flow smoothly. If you've been waiting for a loan, it could arrive today.

Friday 29th: There's further good news today. The family will have something to celebrate.

★ ★ ★
MAY
Your Monthly Guide

Once again you enter a public-spirited and ambitious mood. You snap out of your slightly melancholy mood and become an efficient and workaday person.

If there's an election or referendum at this time, you could be working hard at campaigning, canvassing, etc.

You'll be making some new friends around now. Some will arrive in the course of business. But one other person could arouse sexual feelings in you. I'm not sure whether this is a great love of your life, or someone who will not last long in your affections, only to be swiftly followed by someone who does matter – a lot.

So May is lively, vigorous and capable.

WORK. Your everyday work should be fairly straightforward and pleasant at the moment. Most of your ambition seems directed elsewhere.

There could be one annoying little relationship at work. Someone could be teasing you, or implying that you're less competent than you really are. It's no good getting on your high horse about this. You must just be patient.

If you deal with paperwork all day, be careful about losing one document that will cause a great deal of inconvenience. Be as tidy as possible, especially when it comes to taking business papers home with you.

HOME. You won't spend a great deal of time here, as I imagine you'll be out and about a good deal.

If there's a very young child in the household, its noise and general misbehaviour will undoubtedly get on your nerves this month. You know it's unfair of you, but you can't help yourself.

You'll be glad that an older person is now more settled in the right place with the right company. There could be some contact from a very distant relative – someone, even, whom you've never heard of before. Alternatively, if you live in an old house, previous owners may call and pass the time of day.

HEALTH. A good month for health. There seem to be no complications. A further trip to the dentist may be necessary, perhaps to correct a mistake he made on a previous visit. Don't pay for his mistakes, remember.

MONEY. Your cash flow should be easy and uncomplex. You may be spending other people's money for them, which is always a source of great pleasure! If you sit on a committee, you may be disposing of joint funds, for instance.

A friend may urge you to invest abroad in some way. There could be talk of sharing a holiday home overseas, or investing in a small company. On the whole, allow your Capricorn caution to win over your Capricorn desire to make a fast buck!

If you enjoy gambling, you should pick the three-year-old who will win several of this year's Classics. So bet heavily on your hunch.

LEISURE. Most of your leisure hours will be put into a combined effort to win votes, get the law changed, swing public opinion or support a lost cause!

If you're the sporty type, you will be fascinated by the performance of a particular individual or team: perhaps your home side doing well in soccer or cricket.

If you're artistic, you will enjoy the warmer weather. You can get out and about more, sketching or painting in the countryside.

There are a couple of times this month when you may be mixing business with pleasure. Things will go well, but you wish that your spouse could be more of a help.

LOVE. You could become momentarily infatuated with someone: perhaps someone famous whom you are most unlikely to know personally, perhaps someone touching your life at the moment but basically leading a very different lifestyle to your own.

There's something temporary and fantastic and unreal about this kind of love, and at the time I don't think you'll take it terribly seriously. But it will touch your heart, and make you dream a little!

All this can happen without touching your existing marriage all that much. But there could be one or two events this month that make you realize that perhaps you haven't made the most perfect possible match.

I'll say no more than that!

KEY DATES THIS MONTH

Sunday 1st: You can use other people's advice. After that, you should make up your mind fast and sensibly.

Wednesday 4th: A depressing day, perhaps for no special reason. Maybe it's just your Capricorn nature getting you down.

Friday 6th: Let bygones be bygones, especially if you meet an old enemy. In love you're inclined to feel jealous.

Saturday 7th: It's tempting to spend a lot . . . on little.

Tuesday 10th: Friends will enjoy your company. But at work it's a hard-pressed day, for yourself and others.

Friday 13th: There could be good news about travel. Otherwise, as suits the date, there is a slightly unlucky quality about.

Saturday 14th: You need some solitude, just to collect your thoughts. Someone could act in an aggressive way towards you, making you go back in your shell.

Tuesday 17th: If you are involved in a legal problem, it will soon be solved.

Wednesday 18th: A happy day, especially with kids around. You will smile at your partner instead of criticising.

Saturday 21st: Better weather will cheer you up. If you're keen on summer sports, you'll have a marvellous day.

Sunday 22nd: It's a weekend when you should do your own thing. There could be a temporary cash flow problem.

Monday 23rd: Delay a financial decision for a while. You shouldn't give money to a relative, just to pay off debts.

Wednesday 25th: Listen to your partner; you will reach agreement together. Good day for a trip away from home.

Saturday 28th: Other people, especially in the family, want to go their own way. Let them, leaving you with a good book!

Monday 30th: A marvellous Bank Holiday, though you can't afford a special holiday for all the family.

★ ★ ★
JUNE
Your Monthly Guide

Your marriage comes into sharp relief this month. If you are already married, there may be some cause for anxiety and disappointment in your mind. Some Capricorn people will certainly be contemplating a break-up at this time. Others, more mildly, will be aware of the incompatabilities, always there beneath the surface, starting to confront you.

If you're single but perhaps contemplating marriage, this could be the make-or-break month when either you're jilted,

39

or you bust the engagement up, or you get spliced, or you run away together! The possibilities are endless. It isn't all blissfully happy, but underneath you should be aware of the strength of feeling still between you both.

WORK. Remember the old motto: more haste, less speed. You cannot expect to have everything your own way at work, and however creative you may feel, there will be other people to hold you back, urging caution or actually forbidding you to go ahead with your suggestions.

You will get on the nerves of people at work if you try to hurry them too much. It's worthwhile getting plenty of stock in hand as there could be scarcities ahead.

If you're self-employed, make the most of the favourable influences this June. By bustling, you can earn valuable results.

HOME. Home life has an ambiguous ring to it this month. In one way, as I've already indicated, there could be an anxiety about the state of your marriage. But in another way, you're perfectly happy with domestic arrangements.

If you have children, there could be a special cause for pride this June – perhaps to do with exams, perhaps with sporting achievements at school or college.

If you share your home with another family, there could be some tension, simply over the division of space. Flat-mates will find it hard to get along as easily as you have in the past.

HEALTH. Another broadly healthy month. On the whole, you are a winter person rather than a summer one, and you aren't as crazy about sun-bathing as, say, Leo folk.

Sometimes I feel the Capricorn person has to be forced to enjoy the open air! But this summer looks like being a more relaxed and genuinely hedonistic time for you, and this will be reflected in your general state of health.

MONEY. It's not a notably extravagant month. You may be getting some extra money from a slightly unusual source – perhaps from another country. This will apply particularly if you have relatives or friends abroad, or if you have overseas business interests. But it could apply to almost any Capricornian. Wait and see!

It looks as if one item of expenditure will be removed from your weekly or monthly budget. Perhaps you'll give up smoking, or an HP debt will come to an end.

If you like gambling, I suggest that jockey's colours in gold or orange will be somewhat lucky for you.

LEISURE. You'll be throwing quite a lot of energy into your spare-time activities. You will be more sociable than usual, keen to mix with people at public events. You may go to entertainments that you wouldn't normally visit, events with a touch of exotic glamour: opera, zoos, midnight boating trips, Grand Prix racing.

Inevitably your staid companions will think that you're acting out of character – as, indeed, you will be. They may not like you for this.

LOVE. It's a mixed-up month, but not a depressed time. If anything, you'll realize that you may have repressed in the past feelings that should have been brought out in the open.

I can imagine you getting very up-tight about the sweetheart in your life, and then making passionate love, almost to disprove your inner feelings. You'll tend to blow hot and cold, from one day to the next.

If, as is perfectly possible, you're crazily in love with someone from a very different background, you'll not know whether you're coming or going. But it's an enlivening experience.

KEY DATES THIS MONTH

Wednesday 1st: You may be attracted to the friend of a friend. This could be the start of a slightly guilty liaison.
Thursday 2nd: Anything to do with the general public seems to be lucky at the moment. You could have a feeling for public opinion that proves surprisingly right. Politics could be much on your mind.
Saturday 4th: You have a disappointment, possibly due to someone's ill-health. But you turn your attention to some other hobby or task around the house.

41

Tuesday 7th: A happy day, with the accent on romance and delight in getting to know someone better.

Thursday 9th: You will have difficulty in getting the co-operation of others. If you take part in committee work, you'll be very frustrated by decisions reached.

Sunday 12th: A nice family day, with good flow of sympathy and understanding between the generations.

Wednesday 15th: Children cause some anxiety, especially if they're taking exams. You could have some contact with the police, for some reason.

Friday 17th: Nice weather will make a difference to your weekend plans. If you love camping or caravanning, you should plan a trip away from home.

Saturday 18th: Lucky afternoon, with one favourite jockey of yours having a string of winners.

Wednesday 22nd: Pleasant morning and afternoon, but the evening could be a disaster.

Friday 24th: Someone may be trying to twist your arm, which you resent. But there's good sense in what they want. Perhaps you're being a bit obstructive.

Tuesday 28th: You'll gradually change your mind about a problem, admitting that the impossible could take place.

★ ★ ★
JULY
Your Monthly Guide

This looks like being a long, hot summer for you. Many Capricorn people will be building up a strong passion that will sustain them in the next two or three months.

Your whole desire-nature will be awakened. The most obvious outlet will be sexual, and I would expect there to be someone in your life about whom you will feel very strongly.

But this passion could also be to do with art, music, a sport or other recreational pursuit. It could be attached to the discovery of a brand-new interest in life – anything from astronomy to zoology!

It's noticeable how much more free and easy-going you will be in the next couple of months.

WORK. Keep an eye open for new opportunities, bearing in mind that any change is unlikely to take place this month – or, indeed, in the very near future.

Make the most of opportunities that could lead to promotion in the early autumn. Inside yourself you feel full of confidence and assurance, but others may doubt your readiness or talent to take on the new work. So that's where a delay may occur.

Just remember that, in all sorts of meetings, not simply job interviews, you may assert your own personality a little too strongly for other people's liking. You'll appear a person of power and perhaps arrogance. So cool it. It's wise to hold back some of your forceful personality at the moment.

HOME. At home there will be excitement to see if one member of the family can triumph – in exams, or a sport, or a job interview. Capricorn mothers are full of pride at the moment, and will egg on their children in a real no-holds-barred pushy manner.

Domestic matters won't preoccupy you too much this month. You are keen to be out enjoying yourself, and daily housework will not appeal. Some Capricorn folk lucky enough to have help in the house will find a specially hard-working maid or cleaner who will take a load off your shoulders.

HEALTH. Trust nature! You're moving into a phase of life when natural processes of recuperation and healing are able to work particularly effectively.

Don't hinder them too much by neglecting your beauty sleep, punishing your body too strenuously (through work or sport) or eating bad food at the wrong time.

Rest, proper nourishment and a calm mind are what you need at the moment. If, unhappily, you have suffered any heart trouble recently, this advice is most important.

MONEY. You will spend a good deal of travel, entertaining and clothes this month. It's all part of your anti-puritan, life-loving attitude this summer.

If you have a new sweetheart with whom you're smitten, you could be spending a good deal on your own appearance and in gifts for him or her. If you're a girl, you may well be getting quite a few presents in return. It looks quite a lush, flush time.

Even if you're living a fairly quiet, normal family life, you will still be spending on luxuries – especially garden furniture such as barbecues, patio gear, maybe a tent or caravan.

If you're a gambler, you'll have luck in the second week.

LEISURE. Your whole approach to life is pretty relaxed this month. I think you'll be wanting to spend a lot of time alone with someone you love, which may mean letting the family get on with its own affairs (if you're married) and (if single) neglecting some of your everyday friends in favour of the new boyfriend or girlfriend.

There seems to be a touch of danger in one of your leisure pursuits. It could be the chance to go hot-air ballooning or climbing in beautiful hilly country or sailing in a sea that could get too rough for comfort. But you won't come to any harm.

LOVE. I've already indicated that most of July is a sexy, high-powered time for you, with your libido rising to quite a crescendo of passion as the month progresses.

This can work as much within marriage as outside it. Indeed, even if you are conducting an extra-marital affair at this time, I think you'll still be devoting a lot of bedtime attention to your spouse – perhaps out of guilt, more probably because you are so hyped-up that sexual energy oozes out of you!

KEY DATES THIS MONTH

Saturday 2nd: You will enjoy being in a strange environment. If you go anywhere new, take plenty of photographs to show people back home.
Tuesday 5th: Lock your car, or something could get stolen or damaged. Elderly Capricorn folk should beware of strangers calling at the door.
Wednesday 6th: Watch out for a silly quarrel. It doesn't mean much in itself, but you could see it as an emotional watershed.

44

Saturday 9th: Friends are a joy this weekend. Excellent time to leave on holiday – or steal a few moments with someone you love.

Sunday 10th: If playing sport, there could be some unsporting behaviour. Altogether a day when good manners get forgotten.

Wednesday 13th: You could be lucky in an unusual way. Be nice to someone, and you can make a fresh start together.

Thursday 14th: Another lucky day. If you're a gambler you can win a string of winners. Don't ask me which they are – you're the intuitive one today!

Saturday 16th: A party at the weekend has drawbacks. You may mix with the wrong people. Even so, there are happy links with a couple whom you would like to see again – soon.

Tuesday 19th: There could be criticism behind your back – but as a tough-minded Capricornian you can take it!

Wednesday 20th: If you're worried about an impending visit, relax – it will go splendidly.

Saturday 23rd: An idea at the back of your mind takes concrete shape. Follow it up with optimism. Romance suddenly grabs your attention.

Sunday 24th: Another sexy day when you can discover happiness in the midst of a mundane Sunday.

Thursday 28th: You find happiness again – out of nowhere.

★ ★ ★
AUGUST
Your Monthly Guide

The good times continue. This should be a happy and fulfilling month, whether or not you are in the middle of a lively love affair. You'll feel glad to be alive.

Not everything is sunny, however. If you are conducting a secret romance, people's suspicions will be aroused, even if the whole truth doesn't ever materialise.

There could be a worry about a member of your family – possibly a brother or sister who has not been a great success in life.

The best news, in a way, is the luck you should enjoy this August. The tide is flowing nicely in your favour, and I would expect you to enjoy some good fortune.

WORK. There isn't much to do at the moment. You may be between projects – or, if you have a routine job, the volume of business will be lower than usual at this time of year.

Part of your luck could curiously involve the firm or organisation for which you work. The department could win a prize, perhaps for the work you do but possibly linked to a flower show, cricket competition or other event in which your firm is entered.

On a more practical note, there could be a lot of co-operation now with other firms in the area, leading to joint leisure facilities being made available to your staff.

HOME. There could be concern for a black sheep of the family who has fallen on hard times – yet again! You may have to help out, financially and in other ways.

There could be more contact than usual with a brother or sister. Perhaps one or the other of you is visiting.

You may notice damage to the windows of your home, so repair and redecoration may be called for.

An animal could also be causing damage in the garden. An official complaint may have to be made.

HEALTH. Back-ache, strained muscles and ligaments, and even cartilage trouble are all possibilities if you indulge in too much new or unfamiliar activity. This could be caused in the course of strenuous daily working life, or perhaps sport or, who knows, through too much love-making!

Internally the danger zone is the liver, especially if you have a passion for spicy food and plenty of drink.

None of this means that you will definitely pull a muscle or get liverish – but these are the potential trouble-spots this August.

MONEY. This is a distinctly lucky month for you. A sum of money that's been promised a long time could finally turn up. You could have good fortune at the races or the start of the British soccer season. And a personal friend could be surprisingly – and gratifyingly – generous towards you.

There could be a string of winners at the betting shop. Pick carefully the horses you know, especially those whose progress you've followed through this particular season.

46

You could be a winner on the pools. Not a top dividend, perhaps, but be grateful for smallish mercies!

LEISURE. Your August seems busy and varied, especially if you have guests staying. It's an ideal time to explore your own scenic area, as there could be much more beautiful countryside within a few miles of your house than you've realized in the past.

There could also be several exciting visiting attractions in your district.

You'll have fun, believe it or not, sorting out an attic in your own home or that of an elderly relative who is about to change residencs. This will bring back fascinating memories, and you may unearth several forgotten treasures.

LOVE. Your love life continues to be lively, though I think the overall rhythm is slowing down a bit – at last. This may well have been linked to a happy revival of your existing relationship, be it marriage or steady love partnership.

There are excellent links at the moment with Aquarians and Scorpians.

If you take a holiday together, do remember to take lots of photographs as a memento of this fabulous summer. But at the back of your mind is the thought that the honeymoon-style summer can't last forever.

So enjoy it while it does.

KEY DATES THIS MONTH

Monday 1st: A busy day leads to an enjoyable evening. Be on your guard against revealing a secret – but keep your ears pricked in case you overhear one!

Wednesday 3rd: You'll be irritated with tradesmen who don't deliver the right goods.

Thursday 4th: You'll hear some gratifying news that proves you were right all along.

Friday 5th: This looks an unusual, stimulating day. Your normal Capricorn reserve is not in evidence today.

Saturday 6th: You remain highly unconventional, taking risks and enjoying doing so.

Wednesday 10th: A trip with companions will be a great

success, except for one disagreeable incident. Don't rush to conclusions on the flimsiest of evidence.

Friday 12th: An important day in business. You'll get your own way – but only after plenty of patient negotiation.

Saturday 13th: A break in routine is called for. Go somewhere new, but keep an eye on mischievous youngsters!

Wednesday 17th: A marvellous day. A surprise turns up out of the blue. A romance could blossom in secret.

Friday 19th: The start of the right weekend to see distant members of the family – or bump into old friends on holiday.

Monday 22nd: You'll hear an interesting suggestion – not applicable to your life at present, but store it at the back of your mind.

Wednesday 24th: Good day for reaching agreement with others. Quite an amiable love life; you have lots of laid-back charm.

Friday 26th: A partner may not be feeling one hundred per cent at the moment. You will feel concerned and sympathetic.

Sunday 28th: There could be a special event in your neighbourhood that will give much pleasure and fun.

Tuesday 30th: Be patient with the very young . . . and very old!

★ ★ ★

SEPTEMBER
Your Monthly Guide

This looks a slightly more sombre month. Bad news somewhere in your life could mean that you must drop your easy-going summertime mood and become a rather more serious, responsible member of society once again.

I mustn't exaggerate this change of mood. Undoubtedly it will be marked for some Capricornians, but others will simply notice a slight change in outlook: a desire to be more ambitious at work, an inner realization that you cannot trust to luck.

Some Capricorn folk will have a stroke of bad luck, though it won't be entirely unexpected. I'm thinking about the illness or possible death of an elderly relative or neighbour.

WORK. The work scene gets a bit complicated from now on. I have mentioned the possibility of promotion in your existing job or a total move to another job altogether. There will have been rumours, thoughts at the back of your mind, one or two opportunities along these lines already in the course of 1983.

These take on firmer shape this September. I'm not saying a move will definitely take place. Indeed, your hopes may be raised, only to be dashed in the next month or two.

It could be the arrival of a new boss which will trigger these thoughts in your mind.

HOME. There could be sadness in the family circle – sadness mingled with the thought that change is inevitable and inexorable.

You could join a scheme that's run locally to help you save money – perhaps by shopping regularly at a particular supermarket. On the debit side of this particular coin, you may have to pay the outstanding debts of a member of the family who's run into financial trouble.

There will be encouraging news if you've applied for a government grant to improve your house. A planning application will go through on the nod.

HEALTH. Stay at home if feeling poorly. It's a month when an inherited ailment could manifest itself, or when a contagious illness could quickly be passed between members of the family or colleagues at work.

All the same, September is a broadly recuperative time – especially if you can use your own personality to vanquish an illness. By force of willpower you can tell a virus to shove off – and you'll be successful.

Mumps, measles or chicken-pox could be making the rounds of your neighbourhood just now.

MONEY. This is always an expensive time of year for you, with new activities grabbing your interest as the leisure-hour evenings lengthen. All the same, you know that you must be thrifty. Whether you'll be totally successful here is another matter.

You may be inclined, in true Capricorn spirit, to spend

49

more on older people than children. Not a good time for gambling, though the third week has a couple of lucky days.

If you're going away for a late summer holiday, you may not have anticipated how much it will all cost – and people with whom you're going may not bring enough of their own money.

LEISURE. You should be getting good at a hobby you've taken up in the last month or two. A good time to be doing well in competitions to do with the voice (speech training, singing, acting, etc.).

Something you've neglected will come in useful for somewhere else. I can't be more specific than that! You'll be glad that you don't have to finish a task that had become increasingly unpleasant.

If you play cards such as bridge or whist, there could be a new weekly club or get-together that will become a regular source of fun for you in the weeks ahead.

LOVE. There's a sweet influence encouraging tenderness and love in the early part of the month, but this co-exists with a number of harsher factors encouraging quarrels, separation and dissent.

An existing friendship – especially the one that's been going great guns through the summer – shows some danger of foundering, but there are no clear signs yet of a complete break.

Marriage, if anything, will do better in this kind of situation. A little crisis may draw the two of you closer together.

KEY DATES THIS MONTH

Thursday 1st: A warm-hearted day, lovely for romance. Even if you're happily married, there could be some flirting on the side!

Saturday 3rd: Don't allow spoilt children to spoil your day for you. Be strict, and they'll soon step into line.

Monday 5th: Someone at work will act in an unfamiliar way. There could be a special link with a large city overseas.

Wednesday 7th: With the new academic year starting, you should book up for a daytime or evening class.

Friday 9th: Good weekend to give a small drinks party. You may mix with some well-to-do people, and get a whiff of real luxury.

Monday 12th: You get the chance to be more versatile than usual. Keep competition friendly, or a friend will fall out with you.

Wednesday 14th: A regular service may soon come to an end. If you travel by public transport, they may soon change the timetable to your disadvantage.

Friday 16th: A sight or sound from the past could bring you luck, in a curious way. A journey will take longer than you plan. Lucky numbers: 5, 24, 29.

Saturday 17th: A grand sporting day. You'll have a tune humming in your mind all day. Lovely evening for romance.

Tuesday 20th: If you work in research, you could make a marvellous discovery.

Wednesday 21st: There could be some bad news at home – news that makes you think, at any rate.

Friday 23rd: There may be some bitter medicine to swallow – but it's sugar-coated.

Saturday 24th: An enjoyable day provided you can push other matters to the back of your mind.

Tuesday 27th: Good day for taking a test, or hearing the result of an earlier one. A successful day. You might even win a contest in newspaper or magazine.

★ ★ ★
OCTOBER
Your Monthly Guide

This is quite a crunch month. There may be failure to contend with, or a crowd of money worries, or the danger of just being pipped at the post.

I don't think this need cause great depression, but given that your Capricorn nature is a bit down-beat at the best of times, I doubt whether you're going to be jumping for joy.

At the same time, your great virtue is realism and your greath strength is your stamina, your ability to survive. So you'll grin and bear it, whatever your difficulties may be.

I don't want to suggest that anything very terrible will

happen. But your high hopes of earlier this year will be somewhat lowered.

WORK. At work there's the likelihood that a promised promotion will not now take place. If you were going in for a more senior post within the same company, you may be beaten by a close rival – someone whom you don't think is as talented as yourself.

Capricorn wives may find this state of affairs affecting their husband's careers rather than their own.

Two other points to note: (1) following on this development, there could be a ray of hope for the future – in 1984. So keep your fingers crossed. And (2) you'll be much more circumspect about whom you'll talk to, freely, at work.

HOME. The sense of partial failure that afflicts this month could affect your home life, too. There could be some illness still within the family circle. There could also be a lack of money in the family kitty.

I suppose that a grown-up son or daughter, still living at home, could be made redundant. Or you may be expected, perhaps unexpectedly, to contribute towards the further education of a child – your own, perhaps, or else a nephew, niece or godchild.

There could be some damage in the garden, caused by vandals or bad weather.

HEALTH. Beware of early autumn sore throats, laryngitis or even the mumps that were around last month and you've never suffered from this infection.

Most Capricorn folk aren't great drinkers. Even so, please note that a lot of alcohol will disagree with you this October even more than usual.

Good month for being a blood donor, especially if you belong to a rare blood group for which there's a shortage.

MONEY. You have a lot of money worries this October, which is unusual inasmuch as you're normally an organized person. You may not be rich, but you know how to run your finances.

Obviously some of the muddle could arise from the arrival of several unexpected demands on your resources: the need to help someone out of a scrape, to do emergency repairs on your home or car, or perhaps the necessity to pay for something which you thought would be free – or paid by the organisation you work for.

It's not really a lucky month for gambling.

LEISURE. You can spread a lot of happiness this October by being natural, especially among older people who value your company.

An opportunity to go abroad may crop up, but there'll be others to think of, and the expense will be considerable.

Don't be put off a leisure activity just because you've never done anything like it before. If you've never danced on stage, or acted in a dramatic group, or done a maintenance course on motors, or learnt poker – have a go now!

There could be one friend who's trying to liven up your life, but you aren't really similar in outlook. It'll be hard to put this person down – gently.

LOVE. This is not a deeply passionate month. Some Capricornians will have kissed a sweetheart goodbye, never to see each other again. For others, the relationship may have been quietened down, or put into cold storage for a while, perhaps because others were getting suspicious.

With a marriage there are too many practical worries for you to work up a good head of romantic steam. You'll go a bit solitary.

Good links still with Aquarians and Scorpians, but there isn't quite the magic there was.

KEY DATES THIS MONTH

Saturday 1st: There could be a surprise around the shops. If you eat out, you'll have a wonderful time in the right company.

Monday 3rd: At work there's a question-mark over someone's future. Some interesting social ideas are mulling round at the back of your mind.

Thursday 6th: Keep plans simple, especially if meeting people in strange places.

Friday 7th: You should feel happy but tired, with a glow of achievement. You'll be buoyed up by happy news elsewhere.

Saturday 8th: A cheerful family weekend, though you can't get work problems out of your mind.

Wednesday 12th: A key day for your career. If you were hoping for success, you may just be pipped at the post.

Thursday 13th: Good links with Gemini and Aquarius folk.

Friday 14th: Money worries crowd in on you. You will be worried about a loan that has to be repaid.

Monday 17th: You may be very busy on the phone, trying to get people, banks, etc. to co-operate. It won't be easy.

Wednesday 19th: An entertainment in your area is exactly what you need – but it's expensive, and you're not sure you've got time. Go anyway!

Friday 21st: You must get the right balance between responsibility and interference. With a child you must allow the youngster to have a say in his or her future.

Saturday 22nd: Nice for sport, nasty for shopping. You'll be happier with friends than family.

Sunday 23rd: Someone may not come up to your expectations. You're inclined to be a bit of a snob at the moment.

Wednesday 26th: Don't say 'yes' to a plan unless you understand all the details.

Saturday 29th: A better weekend. It looks a happy, sociable time.

★ ★ ★

NOVEMBER
Your Monthly Guide

It's a more cheerful scene that greets you in November. You'll be passing on a cheering message to others, and in return you'll hear of a promise, a hop or perhaps a compliment.

Life won't be so bad after all.

It's a month when it pays to be proud of yourself and your accomplishments . . . but not pompous into the bargain.

It's possible that you'll be going back to your roots in some way, which will be fascinating for you but not so interesting for the people around you.

There will be an air of reconciliation in your personal life. If there have been angry silences or cross words with a relative – whether your spouse or child – things are better now.

WORK. There's a better atmosphere at work, too. After the disappointment of last month will come an effort by your boss and yourself to make the best of a bad job. Your existing job will be changed somewhat to give you a bit more initiative. And there may be an added responsibility that's small to start with, but promises well for the future.

Some Capricorn folk, desperate to raise money quickly, will have taken a part-time job in the evenings or weekends. This sounds boring, but in fact it'll turn out to be more fun than sweat.

HOME. There's a sweeter air at home, too. If there's been a finger of suspicion pointed recently, now's the time to kiss and make up. If a child has been acting rebelliously, trying to prove something to himself, there can now be a greater degree of trust and understanding between you.

If you have had any repair work done around the house, you'll have to call the workmen back again – particularly plumbers. One craftsman will almost certainly criticise another, saying he's no good!

An elderly relative has a bright idea about Christmas or the New Year festivities which you'll like very much.

HEALTH. There's gradually a change in your psycho-physical system in the course of November. The signs are that you've been a bit under the weather during October and early November; but this low-spirited time is drawing to a close.

In the first part of the month you're a bit at odds with yourself, inclined to give way to a small but troublesome illness. It may be one that you successfully put to one side in October, only to have it reappear now.

Towards the end of November you become a fighter once more, and should succeed in throwing off this new bout of ill-health.

Some Capricorn people may be damaging their well-being by the fit of their clothes, especially shoes. If a shirt is too tight around the neck, for instance, you could be restricting circulation.

MONEY. You are doing as well as possible, which is better than nothing. Extra funds should now be flowing in.

Pay bills promptly, if possible. There's a chance that one of them – or your bank statement itself – could contain an error in your favour, so check carefully.

Beware of a tempting overseas offer, especially if made personally to you by a dubious individual.

Be more generous in giving pocket-money. It's a good month to spend on home and family.

Resist an obsessive interest in gambling, even bingo. You're tempted to throw too much energy into money-making activities at present, and to assess people's worth too much in terms of their financial worth.

LEISURE. You will enjoy catching up on correspondence, particularly with Christmas coming near. You would like to be more generous than usual this Yuletide, giving little gifts to a number of people who would normally receive nothing from you.

You may also be busy helping a child forward in his studies. You will be learning yourself, so there's a gain for you.

If you have an evening part-time job, this will bring you into contact with some new people – rather different from yourself, but interesting to talk to.

LOVE. Nothing to report. A quiet, amiable month!

KEY DATES THIS MONTH

Wednesday 2nd: There could be a problem at work, with a delay or silence on a key issue. If you're ambitious, there will be considerable frustration at this time.

Saturday 5th: Nice for an evening out with friends. There may be the chance to mix business with pleasure.

Monday 7th: A particularly nice day. There could be good news through the post.

Tuesday 8th: Excellent day for sustained effort – at home or work. But a child could be ill.

Thursday 10th: Another fine day for making your mark in the eyes of others. You'll be lucky if you want to have a flutter.

Saturday 12th: Don't worry too much about the details; it's the overall picture that's important. There could be a muddle over papers, tickets, etc.

Monday 14th: A kind day, quiet but loving. You may be invited somewhere new.

Thursday 17th: There could be a slight upset to your plans. There could be a big rush at the last moment.

Saturday 19th: Don't expect much of a routine day – all sorts of funny little circumstances will occur to delay and amuse you.

Wednesday 23rd: Happiness steals over you. A beautiful face, or the sight of a child's smile will make all the difference to your outlook.

Thursday 24th: There's one small disappointment – otherwise everything goes according to plan.

Friday 25th: You may tell a small lie, just to avoid a quarrel. You'll be glad to see friends as well as family.

Sunday 27th: A visit will work out well. You must start your Christmas preparations in earnest.

Wednesday 30th: At work there's a scurry, with the boss on the rampage. You're not worried by the flap.

★★★
DECEMBER
Your Monthly Guide

It looks a cheerful but fairly uneventful ending to the year. You'll be back on an even keel, after some of the emotional instabilities back in the summer. You'll be happier about your job, glad to enjoy the same old home-life, and probably enjoying a rather better social life than you've managed for a while.

Your mood is cheerful, as I say, but watchful. You don't altogether trust the circumstances around you. You're keeping a special eye on someone – probably your boss – who has given you a promise you intend him to keep.

Romance is friendly and fairly passionate, and your roving eye has returned, just in time for the party season!

WORK. You won't be terribly busy in the weeks running up to Christmas, but you must still put in a lot of hours. This could restrict the time available to you for Christmas preparations, which is rather boring.

You will attend one Christmas treat organised by your

firm. You'll find this enjoyable, so much so that plans will be laid to have similar gatherings regularly in the months to come.

If you work in education or the social services, there will be one alarm in the first week: a cry from the heart which you simply must answer, whatever your professional duties.

HOME. It will be a happy Christmas, with the family in full attendance. A real traditional Christmas with all the trimmings. You'll enjoy yourself.

In the weeks leading to the festivities, you'll have a couple of practical problems on your hands. You may have to help find some temporary living quarters for a member of the family who is momentarily homeless.

And a child will be a bit troublesome, especially if it's teething. There could be some sleepless nights for young married Capricornians.

HEALTH. Apart from a brief illness in mid-month, you look remarkably healthy.

You won't be getting as much physical exercise as you need. Try to put aside some minutes a day, either morning or evening, for some gymnastics or yoga. Simply playing a little sport at the weekends is not enough.

You're also inclined to eat a lot of starch and stodge at this time of year. Try to get your protein and calorie intake from foods which are healthy and wholesome in themselves.

MONEY. Your financial problems won't go away, but they're lessening all the time.

You have a couple of lucky moments this month, though whether they will coincide with horse-races or whatever I can't say. Lucky numbers throughout the month are 2 and 9.

You will receive one unexpected Christmas gift that will be worth quite a lot.

LEISURE. You could be taking part in a Christmas entertainment. No need to be embarrassed, especially if you're working back-stage. Everything from your point of view will go well.

If you're taking part in a contest, such as darts at the pub, you may not be so lucky. Sport this December is a little unlucky. There could even be a pulled muscle or cracked rib if you play a contact-sport.

Social life around Christmas will be everything you desire. Try to go to parties where you will see one or two new faces.

LOVE. Sexually you look as though you're getting interested in life again! There will be an air around you that's attractive and appealing. People will find you a popular figure, and this in itself will arouse your libido.

There could be some hanky-panky, if you've been married for quite a few years, between yourself and your spouse and another couple. I don't say it will actually be wife-swapping, but there will certainly be some interest shown.

If you're young and fancy-free and the affair earlier this year came to nothing, then a brand-new romance could be starting this Christmas and New Year, perhaps with someone whom you don't especially like at first sight.

Persevere and you'll find there are many factors in common between you.

KEY DATES THIS MONTH

Thursday 1st: An unexpected visitor stays longer than you want. You'll be upset by someone with dirty habits.

Saturday 3rd: There could be a disappointment around the shops, which may already be out of Christmas stock.

Sunday 4th: The family will be tetchy, and you'll be glad to go off on your own somewhere.

Wednesday 7th: Neighbours should be in a specially friendly mood. Work and play get muddled up. You could be working some peculiar hours this week.

Saturday 10th: An early Christmas party will be good fun. If you visit a member of the family, there will be some strange news.

Tuesday 13th: You must take a decision that could affect the future of yourself or your immediate family.

Friday 16th: You are a little vulnerable to colds and sneezes – just before Christmas! Put a stop to them now, by going to bed now.

Saturday 17th: You get on well with someone from a different age-group. The two of you can have a splendid time together.

Wednesday 21st: You will share a success at work. In an office party you strike up an exciting friendship. Will it last?

Friday 23rd: The Christmas spirit will suddenly make an impression on you. There could be a surprise visit.

Saturday 24th: You could do with some help in the house! All your plans and treats will work wonderfully.

Sunday 25th: A happy day, a mixture of good food, smiling faces and a treat out in the evening.

Monday 26th: There's some surprise gossip. If out in the afternoon, you have a lucky break – or a narrow escape.

Tuesday 27th: At the sales you'll get something you want – and a couple of things you don't!

Saturday 31st: A marvellous ending to the year, with happiness and high hopes for 1984.

THE WORLD
IN 1983

Politics

There could be a General Election in Britain – in May. I'm
not sure, as it would seem more likely in 1984. If it does take
place, there will be no overall party in charge. The new
government will be a coalition between Conservatives,
Liberals and Social Democrats.

Peter Shore will be the new leader of the Labour Party.

Skirmishes will break out on the border between China and
the USSR. There will be prolonged ground fighting, with
limited air support, but it will not develop into nuclear war.

There will be further erosion of the Soviet control over
eastern Europe. Romania will be in open revolt against
Russia, trying to become neutral like Austria.

There will be a new government in New Zealand. Australia
will be wracked with political dissension, with a new party –
along the lines of the British SDP – being formed.

City riots will break out against the Republican administration in the USA. For the Democrats, Ted Kennedy will be
active – but the dangerous time for him, as far as an assassina-
tion attempt is concerned, is not this year but next.

For the Republicans, the race to the White House will have
started already. Vice-President George Bush will be chal-
lenged by former astronaut John Glenn.

★ ★ ★
The Economy

The world economy will be gathering strength after the
recession of the last few years. This will lead to more
inflation, which will run between 15 and 20 per cent in the
western world.

61

Employment figures will stay as large as ever. Several countries will introduce a sort of civil conscription to keep out-of-work youngsters out of mischief.

The price of oil will top 50 dollars a barrel, but there will be no shortage. Big strides will be taken in the development of an electric-powered car. There will also be a breakthrough in lasers tapping solar energy, bringing long-term free energy a step nearer.

The centre of the economic stage will continue to move east – to Singapore, China and Japan. There will be a special alliance between China and Japan that will have far-reaching technical consequences.

Improved food production in Africa and South America will mean less hunger in the world.

★ ★ ★
Social Trends

Money is on the way out. More bank accounts, credit cards and computerised check-out counters will mean that notes and coins won't be required nearly so much.

Overseas holidays will be as popular as ever, thanks to a new generation of cheaper-to-run aircraft. Vacations in Africa will be appealing, as well as Sri Lanka and India.

Fashions will be brief and sexy, with lots of leg and wild, long hair styles – maybe down to the waist!

★ ★ ★
Natural Events

The Jupiter effect continues to dominate the sky. This means that a number of planets are gathered in one sector of the heavens. While some people feel this will produce great natural catastrophes, I believe the opposite. Jupiter will bring long, hot weather to the northern hemisphere, boosting crops.

But a series of hurricanes in the Caribbean will wreak havoc among the West Indies and the American mainland. Florida and New Orleans will be badly hit.

There will be terrible flooding in the Calcutta region. Earthquakes will shake all down the Euro-Asiatic fault – from Iran to Japan.

★★★
Sport

America will start to play a significant part in the world soccer scene. The European leagues will adopt the free-n-easy USA rules, with more goals and less defensive play.

Top British clubs will be Southampton, West Ham and – inevitably – Liverpool. The FA Cup will be won by a Midlands club.

One marvellous three-year-old will pick up three of Englands Classic races, and then take the Arc de Triomphe in Paris.

English floodlit cricket will become more popular, and, wonder of wonders, Yorkshire will win one of the summer trophies.

In tennis the grip of John McEnroe will be weakened by a bright new star – probably from California but possibly Australia.

★★★
Royal Family

The Prince and Princess of Wales will tour the world in 1983, with special emphasis on the Far East, including China. The main purpose will, naturally, be to show the flag. China and Britain will have reached agreement over the long-term future of Hong Kong, and Charles will be anxious to cement this new-found friendship with China.

The Queen will be involved in a dilemma over Europe. Possibly the President of the EEC will be acting in too political a manner, and public opinion will be swinging towards a non-political head of state for Europe – namely, the Queen.

One of Princess Margaret's children may marry. Prince Andrew will have a narrow escape from a dangerous sport.

YOUR BIRTHDAY HOROSCOPE

This book is designed for everyone born between December 22 and January 20. I have tried to make it as personal to your life as possible, but inevitably there will be a number of questions about your personal life that this book cannot answer.

Without doubt, the best course of action if you want further advice on your life ahead is to apply for your own Birthday Horoscope. This 20-page report is written for you, and you alone. It will be based entirely on your own birth details, right down to the minute of birth (if you know it!) and so will be unique to you and not shared by all other people of the Capricorn star sign.

This report will concentrate first on the broad trends in the next twelve months, covering in greater detail the areas of work, home and family, romance and so on. You may ask questions, though I can't promise to answer every one! All in all, a wonderful insight into your personality and future.

When this service was launched last year, many readers took advantage of this offer and were delighted with the results.

The price of this service is £6.00 in Great Britain, or £7.50 for airmail anywhere in the world. If you live abroad, please pay by International Money Order or bank draft – in £ sterling. Apply direct to me, Roger Elliot, for your individual report, giving your name and address and the date, month, year, place and time (if known) of birth. Delivery will be about three weeks, and be assured that it will receive my personal attention. Send to Starlife, Cossington, Bridgwater, Somerset TA7 8JR, England.